Lawn Care
Business Guide:

The Definitive Guide to Starting and Running Your Own Successful Lawn Care Business

Patrick Cash

www.LawnBusinessResources.com
www.LawnCare-Business.com
www.LawnProSoftware.com

Acknowledgements

I'd like to thank a few people, without whom my success would not be possible.

To Miranda—Your love and support push me to new heights.

To Mom—Without the great upbringing you gave me, I wouldn't be who I am today.

To Keith—Thanks for believing in me, even when I doubted myself.

Table of Contents

Chapter One:

Getting Started

"The way to get started is to quit talking and begin doing."

-Walt Disney

Why Get Into the Lawn Care Industry?

I cannot think of another industry that offers as much growth potential as the lawn care industry. You can start off with just yourself and one mower. If you work smart and are a good marketer you can grow a lawn care business just about as big as you would ever want to.

New customers are constantly being created for you. Think about it:

Have you ever noticed all the new homes and businesses being built? Every one of these is a potential new customer for you. Every time a new home is built that is one more person who needs their lawn taken care of. Every time a new business is built they will need someone to maintain the property.

If you will market smart and work hard there's no reason at all, after the first season of running your business, you would not be <u>turning away</u> work. I've seen time after time where people literally have more work than they can get to. Will this be you? I have no way of knowing this because I don't know you. You may not want to work that hard. You may only want to work part-time. Either way, the possibilities are endless in this industry. It's all up to you!

No matter what your schedule or time commitment to this business, don't limit yourself to just mowing. I have included other add-on businesses you can do to boost your profits year round. For more information on this, see Chapter 6.

How Much Could You Make?

How much you can make depends on several things:
- Where are you located?
- How much competition is there in your area?
- What services do you offer?
- What are you charging for your time?
- How much do you want to work?
- What does the weather allow?

Let's look at each of these for a minute.

Where are you located?

Where you are located affects you in two ways:

The first is population. Obviously if you live where there are a million people in a given area, you'll have more opportunity to have more customers. This still doesn't mean you can't make a great living in a smaller market. Being in a smaller market has its advantages, too. Smaller markets may not have the competition you face in a large city. Each area is going to have its advantages and disadvantages. Be sure to check out your market, competition, etc. and make it work for you.

The second is your mowing season. Depending on the area of the country you are in, you may have a shorter mowing season than in other areas. For example, the mowing season up north is several weeks shorter than in the south. If you live in an area where winters are longer and your loss of income from mowing is unbearable, check out other ways to make money in the off-season. I would definitely suggest that you look into

14

snow plowing during the winter. This more than makes up for the shorter growing season for most companies!

How much competition is there in your area?

Competition is everywhere. You shouldn't worry about it, but instead let it be a motivator. If you didn't have competition, that would worry me. Competition can be a good thing. There are a lot of times I pick up new customers because the competition has done a bad job! If nothing else, the fact that there is competition means that there is money to be made!

What services do you offer?

What services you offer can have a huge impact on your earnings. When you start out you may just want to mow. That's fine, but you can certainly grow your business by offering additional services to your customers. Among other services, you can offer fertilization, aeration, overseeding, fall leaf clean up, landscaping, installation of low voltage lighting, and many more. I discuss these in greater detail in Chapter 6 later in the guide. When it comes down to the wire, the more services you offer, the more money you can earn.

What are you charging for your time?

It is my opinion that everyone should have a minimum charge. You shouldn't unload your equipment for less than this minimum. Set this amount based around the principle that if you work for less than your minimum charge, you're losing money. It costs a certain amount to block off time, drive to a site, load and unload equipment, etc. This costs you time, gas, and wear-and-tear among other things. There are also opportunity costs associated with accepting a job. You could be making more money somewhere else!

You could also be working yourself to death for no substantial profit. If you're working 80 hours a week but aren't charging enough, you won't make any money. It's that simple. You'll just end up worn out, frustrated, unsuccessful, and unhappy. I suggest you charge approximately $1 per minute for every minute you are working (I go into this in more depth later in the guide, but this will give you a starting point).

How much do you want to work?

I realize some people only get into this part time to make extra money. There's nothing wrong with this but if you want to make a serious income you're going to have to put in some time to make it happen. You can use rainy days as your off time. If it is possible, I would recommend working every day it is not raining (excluding weekends).

What does the weather allow?

The weather should average out over a year's time, but from week to week it can make your life a little difficult. This is one major aspect of the business that is totally out of your control. As I'm writing this, we've had three straight days of rain and are in the path of a hurricane that is supposed to make landfall in the next 36 hours.... basically we've lost a week's worth of mowing time. Could I get mad? Sure. Will it help? Nope, not one bit.

Just try and make the best of the weather and use any down time to do some marketing. Also, try to make yourself plan ahead for these times and work extra hard to catch back up afterwards. This way the impact to your business and your finances will be minimal.

Setting and Achieving Goals

Please don't skip over this section! It is very important and could make a huge difference in your personal and business life.

Setting and achieving goals is huge to me, as it should be to you. I set daily, weekly, monthly, yearly and long term goals. Once you start setting small goals and achieving them you will find it to be a great way to literally map out your success in life. Don't get bogged down thinking about how complicated setting goals can be. It's really very simple. Here are the basic rules: Goals need to be written down, they need to be precise, they need to have a time attached to them, and they need to be achievable.

That's it. No complicated formulas or equations...pretty simple, huh?

Let's start with a small example. Say you set a goal to get four new customers each and every week. This may mean you have to put out 200 door hangers or flyers and actually talk to 30 potential customers. Here is how you would put this in "goal form":

"Over the next 52 weeks, I will get four new regular customers for my lawn care business every week.
I will accomplish this by putting out 200 door hangers and by talking to at least 30 potential customers either in person or over the phone."

Your goals can be written on several sheets of paper and in several different formats—just figure out what works best for you. Personally, I make one sheet for daily goals, one for weekly goals, one for monthly goals, etc. There's no limit or minimum for the goals. You can have 100 goals for the next 30 days or you can have one large goal. It all depends on the purpose and the situation. Just keep in mind that goals are something to <u>reach</u> for. Don't set them too low—make yourself work!

Don't get discouraged if you don't meet all of your goals in the time frame you have set. If you don't quite make one but you are making progress toward that goal, simply mark off the ones you have accomplished and move the ones you haven't conquered on to your new sheet.

One important thing to remember about goals is that you have to refer back to them. Actively work to achieve them and chart your progress along the way. I keep my goals written down and I refer to them EVERY DAY. You should too.

For resources on this topic, please visit:
www.LawnBusinessResources.com

What Type of Business Should You Be?

When setting up your business entity, you have several types to choose from. There are three major categories that I would like to cover: sole proprietorship, partnership, and corporation.

I am not giving accounting or legal advice here, and the best bet is to consult with your attorney and/or accountant as to which form may be best for you. What I can do, however, is share what I did and give a summary of some of your choices.

When I started out in this business, we were simply a sole proprietorship. This means that everything was in my name. Our checking account, the business licenses, etc. were all in my individual name. This is, by far, the simplest form of doing business, but may not be the best for all situations and businesses. In this section, I will briefly summarize the three categories.

Sole Proprietorship

Sole proprietorships are for small businesses with only one owner. If you are a sole proprietor, the law doesn't recognize a difference between the things that you own (personal property) and the things that your business owns, which are called assets.

What does this mean to you? It means that the equipment you use to maintain lawns, the trailer on which you haul it, etc. belongs to you in the same way that your television set or microwave oven does.

There's also no legal difference between the money you owe people and the money your business owes people, which are called debts. If you owe someone money for business purposes and the business goes bankrupt, you personally are fully liable for the business's debts.

Partnership

A partnership is a business that has between 2 and 20 partners. The partners all own a piece of the business together and share in the liability, profits, losses, decision-making, etc.

If you want to start a partnership, I recommend that all partners sign a written agreement prepared by a lawyer. At a minimum, the agreement would need to include these points:

• If the partnership ends, what is going to happen to the assets of the business (for example, the equipment and customers)?

• How will the money be shared? Who will control it? (For example, one partner may work every day and another partner may only work on weekends. They would not want to share the profits equally because one partner has contributed more than the other. The same goes for initial investment. If one partner contributes 70% of the initial investment, they would expect to receive more benefit than the other partners). Keep in mind that profits, losses, equipment, etc. may all be shared in different percentages.

• What will happen if one of the partners dies or wants to leave the partnership? In general, I suggest that any and every time a new partner joins, all of the partners sign a new partnership agreement.

You can write your own contracts for a partnership

or use templates found online, but they need to be reviewed by an attorney to make sure that they are valid and legally binding business contracts.

Company, Corporation, LLC

In a company or corporation the business is a separate legal entity (that is, they are more or less a legal person). Having a business in the form of a corporation can shield you from personal liability for some lawsuits and debts. The company is only liable for its debts, not those belonging to its directors or shareholders. In turn, the directors or shareholders are not liable for the company's debts, unless they have signed a personal guarantee* or are negligent in their personal actions that cause the debt or lawsuit (*most loans will require you to sign a personal guarantee).

On the other hand, a corporation is one of the most expensive, most complicated entities to form. These entities are heavily regulated and must adhere to many strict laws.

There are many more options for your choice of business entity. I suggest that you research this heavily and consult with your lawyer and accountant before selecting a legal form for your business. This is a very important decision and, if made improperly, could be the downfall of an otherwise profitable business.

Taxes

My Legal Disclaimer: I do not provide legal or accounting advice, so you will need to get an accountant to clarify any information for your particular business.

Now that we have that out of the way, there are two items I want to mention as far as taxes go:

1. <u>Income Tax</u>: The type of company you start will impact what kind and how much income tax you will pay. There are many advantages and disadvantages to the different entities when it comes to taxes. This is where an accountant comes in handy. They will tell you what will work out best in your particular situation. In the end, a good accountant doesn't cost you money, they save you money!

2. <u>Sales Tax</u>: In a lot of areas of the country, you do not have to pay sales tax on services. You will need to check your area to make sure this is the case. If it is, and all you are doing is mowing or performing other services, you may not have to worry about collecting taxes from your customers! The only items you have to pay taxes on are materials (mulch, flowers, etc.). To simplify things, you should sit down with an accountant, tell them what you are doing or starting, and let them give you the run down for your area on what you are and are not required to do.

Choosing a Name for Your Business

Naming your business is a very important and long-lasting decision. You don't want to have to go back and change it because you did not fully think it through!

Once you have a name in mind, you need to see if the name you want to use is already in use. The Yellow pages and the classifieds are a great source to see what businesses are in your area. You will also want to make sure the name has not been incorporated or registered already (no, you cannot use the name TruGreen, even if there is not one in your area!).

I suggest that you do not use your own name for your business name. If you ever decide to sell your business to a partner or to another private party, they will not want to own a business under someone else's name. This tells them they are going to have to go through the hassle of changing the name, notifying customers, etc., which can be a major turn-off to potential buyers. On the other hand, what if someone bought your business and ran it into the ground or got into trouble? They would be ruining your good name all because the business was named after you. Please just think twice before doing this. Remember that you want your business name to convey professionalism and to be easy to remember. This is another reason not to use your name in the title!

Let's look at two examples: "Dave's Lawn Care" and "Quality Cuts Lawn Care".

You immediately get a perception of the types of work they do. "Dave's Lawn Care" sounds like it was rushed without a lot of insight involved in choosing it. It sounds like a small, unprofessional mowing service. Potential customers may picture "Dave" as a guy with an old push mower in the back of his car doing cheap work. That may sound extreme, but chances are the name "Dave's Lawn Care" will not impress most people.

The name "Quality Cuts Lawn Care" evokes thoughts of quality and reliability. Heck, it even has "quality" right in the name! Do you get a sense of more professional lawn service technicians, good equipment, and a beautiful lawn? You get the point!

On the next couple of pages are some names and slogans you might want to use for your business (please check that they are not currently being used before deciding on one!):

<u>Names:</u>

Blow and Go
Mow Blow and Go
Mow n Go
Green Side Up
Two Fat Guys Mowing
One Man and a Goat
A Cut Above
Alien Lawn Care, "Service that's out of this world"
Better Lawns and Gardens
The Lawndromat, "Neat, Clean, and Green!"
The Lawn Rangers
Progressive Lawn Maintenance
Clean Cut
Green Grass, Inc.
The Grass Barber
Personal Lawn Care

LawnWorks
Yard Smart
Cutting Edge Lawn Care
Down to Earth Lawn and landscape
Ground Control
Leisure Time Lawn Care
Miracle Lawn Mowing, "If it's done right, it's a Miracle Lawn"
The Grass is Greener
Mighty Mow
Easy Green
Greens Keeper Lawn Care
Lawn and Order
Mow, Hoe, and Blow Lawn Service
Green, Greene, and Greener
Who Did It Lawn Service
Lawn Sharks
Lawn Gators
Turf Surfers
Almost Perfect Landscaping
Moe Loenz
The Three Amigos Landscaping
Barber of the Grass
The Lawn Stylist
Grass Hoppers
Executive Lawn Care
Dalmatian Lawn Care, "We don't miss a spot!"
From the Ground Up
Landscaping Workshop
Root Bound
Classic Gardens
Cut Right
Cutting Edge Grass Busters

Pro-Lawn
Pro-Landscape
Copper Valley Landscaping
Island Breeze Lawn Care
Weedaway Lawn Care
Rainmaker Irrigation and Sprinklers
Lawncrafters
Earthworks
April Showers Lawn Care and Landscaping
Creekview Lawn Care
Cut Right
Greenscapes
Oasis Lawn Care
Green and Clean
Clean and Green

Slogans:

"Satisfaction Guaranteed or Double Your Grass Back"
"We Don't Just Cut Grass, We Manicure Lawns"
"Your Yard Barber!"
"Professional Lawn Mowing"
"Your Lawn is My Business"
"The Grass May Be Greener on the Other Side, But it Still Has to be Mowed!"
"Creating Curb Appeal"
"Quality Service from the Ground Up"
"So-and-So Landscaping"
"Beautifying Our Country, One Lawn at a Time"
"Call Us if You Need Your Weeds Whacked"
"Quality is at the Roots of Our Business"
"You'll Get 'Mow' for Your Money!"
"Got Grass?"

"We are the Salon for your Lawn"
"Where Service is Always in Season"
"Taking Care of Your Yard so You Can Do Other Things!"

Creating a Logo for Your Business

Don't short-change yourself by skimping on a logo for your business. Having a logo makes your business appear more professional and helps you stand out from the competition. Think about it—can you name a well-known professional business that does not have a logo? Furthermore, you notice many businesses simply because of their logo or may recognize their logo before you can recall their name. You want your potential customers to have that recognition of your business, too!

You don't have to have art or drawing skills to get a logo. There are a lot of places that will do a logo for you for under $100 (which is well worth it!). Tell them what you have in mind and what colors you would like to use and they will do the rest.

Here are a few logos I have done:

We'll be your lawns best friend

We work hard so you don't have to!

Let us work some magic on your lawn.

Business and Other Licenses

You'll need to get a business license for your business. You may have to have a city license for each city you will be working in as well as a county license. What kind of license you will need depends on what the local municipalities require. For instance, in our area you are required to have a license for lawn care and a different license for landscaping. You will need to clarify this with your local authorities.

All licenses I am aware of have to be renewed every year. While you may be tempted to work without a license, I would suggest you get them as soon as you can so you will be a legitimate business. In some areas the fines for not having the license are much more than it would have cost you to get the license to begin with.

As a special note, if you are planning on working with herbicides or pesticides: In all areas that I am familiar with, you will have to have a state license to perform this service. In addition, you may need to take classes and or take a test to get licensed.

Business Insurance and Bonding

Business Insurance

I really, very strongly suggest that you get insurance. I know small business owners who operate without it, but I feel that they are just asking for trouble. As an example, our business policy covers the business and equipment, and I have separate policies for my truck and trailer.

One good, simple reason to be insured is for your peace of mind. Knowing that if something goes wrong you are covered takes a load of stress off. A second good reason to purchase insurance is that 99.9% of commercial bids will require proof of insurance.

In general, I suggest that you get a $1,000,000 liability policy as a minimum. Depending on who you get coverage with, you may have to get a separate policy if you do landscaping and lawn care. As an estimate, you can expect to pay between $200 to $1000 a year for the lawn care policy and a little more for a landscaping policy. I am not endorsing any company, but quite a few businesses I know of use Hartford Mutual or State Farm for their liability policy. This may be a good place for you to start your insurance search.

Health Insurance

Health insurance is something we all need, but it can be very expensive. If you have to buy it out of pocket (in other words, if you are self-employed and can't get health insurance through your spouse's place of employment) be prepared to spend $500.00 or more a month for decent coverage. Your best bet, as I mentioned above, is if your spouse (if you are married) can get it through his or her employer.

Workman's Comp insurance

Workman's Comp is insurance for any employee that may get hurt on the job. Again, talk to your insurance agent to find the coverage that suits you best. Luckily, the rates for the lawn care industry are a lot lower than in some industries.

Bonds

You shouldn't have to worry about bonds if you're just starting out. Usually to be bonded requires you to have established business practices for at least three years (It is possible to apply for a bond and get underwritten with less than three years in the business).

There are numerous requirements to be bonded on jobs, one of which is that you are "bondable". Bondable actually means that the Contractor's capital, character & capacity have been analyzed by a Surety Underwriter. The Surety Underwriter has then determined that the Contractor can perform certain types of work within established bounds. Based upon that, the Surety Company will issue Surety Bonds guaranteeing the Contractors performance and/or payments within those guidelines.

A surety bond is a three-party instrument between a surety (the company writing the bond), the contractor (you), and the project owner (the person you are doing the work for). The surety binds the contractor to comply with the terms and conditions of a contract. If the contractor is unable to successfully perform the contract, the surety assumes the contractor's responsibilities and ensures that the project is completed.

When might you need to be bonded? If you were doing large landscape installations, for instance, you would probably be required to be bonded.

How to Accept Credit Cards Easily

In this day and time, it seems that you can't really be in business if you can't accept credit cards. Accepting credit cards will allow customers to spend money more easily with you—which will make their experience more enjoyable and less stressful. This is important for building your customer base.

In order to accept credit cards, you'll need to get what's called a merchant account. You can get a merchant account through your bank, among other places. Let me tell you, though, what we do so that I can accept credit cards over the phone, in my office, out in the field, and over the internet. How can I do all of this? Simple. We use Paypal and their virtual terminal program.

Paypal's virtual terminal will let you accept credit cards from your customers. The rate is about what you would pay to do so from any other merchant account but without a lot of the hassles. I have a quick way for you to sign up on www.LawnBusinessResources.com. Go there to sign up. Once you do that then sign up for a virtual terminal. As of now, this service only costs $30 a month. The money from credit cards goes into your Paypal account, which is similar to a bank account. You can transfer it to your checking account at anytime. If you do enough processing with them, Paypal will even send you a debit card you can use to get money out of any ATM from your Paypal account.

Business Phones

Regardless of the size of your business, you have to have a way for customers to get in touch with you. I think you have a couple of good options for this:

1. You can have a regular phone line that you use for a business. It is best not to share a phone line with your home. This way when the phone rings, you can answer it by the business name. This presents your customer with a more professional demeanor.

2. You can have a cell phone for business purposes and use this as your main number in your advertisements, etc.
Or you can do what we do...

3. I have a business line that is forwarded to my

cell phone. I do this because the phone company will give me a listing in the yellow pages, etc if I have a "business" line. I forward the phone line to my cell because I try to return phone calls as soon as possible. This is a little bit of a hassle and is slightly more expensive, but I really like to have the ability for my phone calls to follow me wherever I go.

No matter your method of obtaining a business phone, try and return your calls as quickly as possible. I have won new customers over a competitor simply because my competitor was too busy to return the phone call. If people don't hear back from someone fairly quickly they will call someone else. Make sure you are the one they can reach.

Always be polite and let the customer do the talking to tell you what they want. I keep a notepad and take notes while I'm talking on the phone. You don't want to show up at a home or business and ask "What was it you wanted a price on?" That is not professional at all and does not give them the sense that their business is important to you.

Business Cards

Business cards are very important. I suggest you get them printed as soon as possible. How are you going to tell someone how to get in touch with you if they are interested in your services?

I'm always on the lookout for the place that has the best deals. If you go to www.LawnBusinessResources.com you can find several places that offer full color business cards at very competitive prices. You can use their stock lawn care backgrounds or you can upload your own.

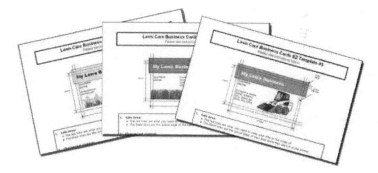

etting a Website

...re a professional lawn care business
...website. Websites are a very low-cost,
...ject of your business success. Your
cus... ...ed to businesses having a website these
days—don't ...point them or drive them away because
you don't. You can use your website as a way to
showcase photos of your work, allow customers to
submit a form to request services, allow customers to
pay their bill online, and more. I can't stress how much
having a professional website can help your business.

For resources on this topic, please visit:
www.LawnBusinessResources.com

Notes:

Chapter Two:

Advertising

"Advertising says to people, 'Here's what we've got. Here's what it will do for you. Here's how to get it.'"

-Leo Burnett

What's a Customer Worth to You?

Before we get going on the advertising section, I want you to think about what a customer is really worth to you. Most people really don't take time to think about this. I want you to figure out what the average customer is worth for your business. For example, if a typical client gets you to mow their lawn 40 times during the season and gets you to do fall leaf removal, I would venture to say that customer is worth about $1800 to you over the course of a year. If an average customer is worth $1800 to you, why on earth would you not be willing to spend a fraction of that to get new ones?

I've talked to business owners who think they can't afford to spend $5 or so to do some sort of direct mail advertising or to pay decent referrals. This is a mistake and a trap! If an existing customer sends you a new customer (who is going to be worth $1800 to you), don't you think you can afford buy that existing customer a $50 gift certificate or give them a few free cuts? If you do, I guarantee you that you and your business will be the first thing they think of when someone mentions needing a lawn care service!

Think hard about this. It can make all the difference in the world to your success!

Advertising-
Ways to Outsmart Your Competition

This section is a compilation of things we have used from time to time to get more business.

Special note: You'll notice in my guide I don't ever mention putting flyers (or anything else) in mail boxes. That's because it's illegal! Don't do it.

In this section we will cover:

- Door Hangers
- Flyers
- Postcards
- Bandit Signs
- Newspaper Ads
- Custom Sticky Notes
- Monthly Newsletters
- T-Shirts
- Setting Up Referral Programs
- Ways of Advertising Your Competition Probably Hasn't Thought Of...

Door Hangers

Door hangers have been the best thing I have found to-date (other than possibly word of mouth / referrals) to get new customers. The main thing I would stress with door hangers is have a place to leave a price quote on them. This separates the "tire kickers" from the serious clients. If you leave a price quote on the door hanger, they already know what you will be charging them. This means that, of the people who call, most will be serious about you and your services.

Below are two pictures we use for door hangers (we also use these for flyers). We came up with these ourselves and they seem to work pretty darn well.

Golfing Weather Is Here But
The Lawn Needs Mowing....

Let Us Help Free Up Your Time So you
Can Do The Things You Want To Be Doing.

We Can Service Your Lawn For Only
$ Per Visit

The Fish Are Biting But
The Lawn Needs Mowing....

Let Us Help Free Up Your Time So you
Can Do The Things You Want To Be Doing.

We Can Service Your Lawn For Only
$ Per Visit

In addition to any you can come up with on your own, there are some other door hangers available online.

For resources on this topic, please visit:
www.LawnBusinessResources.com

46

Flyers

Flyers are okay, but they don't work nearly as well as door hangers, postcards, or referral marketing. In my opinion this is because the door hangers are on the door. They have to remove them to see what they are. I think flyers have been so overdone most people treat them like junk mail.

BUT I have had good luck with one type of flyer (I have included a sample of it on the next page). I made a flyer with tear-off strips (with phone numbers) and put them at two local grocery stores. I couldn't believe it, but I had to put new ones up in less than two weeks.

One good thing about flyers is you can make them yourself on your pc and print them at home, which means there is very little cost tied up in them. If you need to get a lot of them printed, go to your local printing store.

As a last tip on flyers, I do not recommend that you put them out in parking lots on cars. This is generally a wasted effort. Most people get annoyed and throw these away without even looking at them. Additionally, you have no idea where these people live. Even if they did call you, your work would be spread out all over the place!

Lawn Care
Professional, Affordable.
Why spend your time on lawn work
when you could be out doing the
things you enjoy?
Let us take care of all your lawn care
needs.
Mowing
Trimming
Blow off driveways and walkways
Fall leaf removal
And more...
We also offer a "vacation" mowing service. (We can
mow for you while you're gone on vacation!)
Give us a call today!

555-1212 | 555-1212 | 555-1212 | 555-1212 | 555-1212 | 555-1212 | 555-1212 | 555-1212 | 555-1212 | 555-1212 | 555-1212 | 555-1212 | 555-1212

Postcards

Next to door hangers, postcards are my next preferred method of marketing. Why? I think it's probably because postcards deliver information the way people want to get it today ...quickly and with little or no effort. A brief captivating message on a postcard with an enticing offer sent to the right prospects can generate a large number of sales leads.

Keep your postcard simple. Make it look at first glance like a message from a friend instead of an advertisement. This creates a pleasant emotional response from readers even though they quickly realize that it is a commercial message.

State the biggest benefit you offer to customers, then briefly add a few other advantages or features you provide. End with a compelling reason for prospects to contact you.

Tip: You are not trying to close sales directly from a postcard. There's not enough space on a postcard to provide all the information your prospects need to make a buying decision. You just want the potential client to call you. You can close the sale in person!

There are several benefits to using postcards as a marketing source. First, people will read postcards. Almost everyone will read a postcard—even people who usually throw out other direct mail without even opening it. Why is that? Because it's almost impossible to throw out a postcard without at least looking at the message, and there is no work involved to get to the message (unlike opening an envelope). This high rate of readership is the main reason why postcards produce a bigger response than other types of direct marketing.

With other types of direct mail you often lose prospects who need your services but never saw your offer.

Second, postcards are cheap to produce. Postcards can cost less than 2 cents each to produce if you print them using your own computer. You can print postcards individually on blank 4 x 6 inch index cards or print 4 postcards on 8 1/2 x 11 sheets of index card stock and cut each sheet into quarters. Postcards cost between 4 cents and 9 cents each to produce if you use a commercial printing service, depending on the number you have printed and the quality you want.

Third, postcards are cheap to mail. Even the postage for mailing postcards is cheap—currently 27 cents each to send them by First Class Mail in the US. The only requirement for this special rate is that the dimensions of your postcards are at least 3 1/2 x 5 inches (the standard size for postcards) but not over 4 1/4 x 6 inches (jumbo size postcards).

Tip: Always use a real stamp on your postcards. It produces more replies than a printed indicia (imprinted postage) ...probably because people associate a printed indicia with junk mail.

Don't overlook postcards the next time you want to drive a huge amount of traffic to your website or generate a flood of new sales leads. They're simple to use, highly effective and very low-cost.

For resources on this topic, please visit:
www.LawnBusinessResources.com

Bandit Signs

Bandit signs are the signs you see on the sides of the road. I want to include a small section on these signs because some people swear by them and say they work extremely well for them.

With that said, we don't use them and know they are not allowed in some areas. I personally have never stopped and gotten a number off of a sign to call someone about their services. Use these at your own discretion!

Newspaper Ads

Don't take out an ad in just any section of the newspaper. A newspaper ad can be effective, but it needs to be in the right place and be worded properly. Please don't misunderstand, I like classified ads. I just wouldn't suggest that you rely on them to be your only method of advertising. See if your local newspaper has a "business directory" section. This will place your business in the spotlight—not on a page with pets and yard sales! Our local paper has this, and we have run ads in this section with good results.

I think newspaper advertisements have worked for us simply because, for whatever reason, a lot of the other lawn care businesses haven't used it. At the time I wrote this, our ad was one of two or three lawn care businesses in there. This means that we have a 30-50% chance that anyone looking in the newspaper for lawn care will call us first. Keep in mind that the business directory listings work well for additional services, such as leaf removal in the fall as well.

When it comes to wording, keep the ads simple:
Professional Lawn Care Affordable Rates
444-3333

Or
Got Leaves? We'll get them up and leave your lawn neat and clean. Free quote call:
444-3333

This will get the point across but will be simple and will cost you less!

Custom Sticky Notes

I really like these because I believe they have a lot of potential. Custom sticky notes are something we have just started using. We seem to be getting good results with them and they are easy to use. We simply go through a neighborhood and put them on the front door, just like a delivery company does if you are not at home.

Here's an example:

Tired of Spending Your Free Time On Lawn Work?

We can free up your weekends so you can be doing the things you want to do.

Complete Lawn Care
Leaf Removal
Affordable, Reliable Service

Give us a call at:
555-4232

I get these printed locally, but there are a lot of places on the internet that specialize in them. Do a search online for "Custom post it notes".

Start a monthly newsletter

Starting a monthly newsletter is a great way to keep your name in front of your clients (and people you want to become your clients). Newsletters, if they are done properly, make you look very professional. If you are working an area where you know most of the people pay to have their lawns maintained (and you already have a few clients in the area), I would send the newsletters to the entire community. I think newsletters are one of the best ways to maintain a presence with your clients without bugging them like some other forms of advertising do.

T-Shirts

    T-shirts are an excellent advertising tool. They can make your company look a lot bigger and more established than it really is. I generally use yellow with dark green or black ink (this stands out and shows up very well), but any color will work. If you can, have a shirt design that is easily recognizable—even from 20 feet or more away. This allows for potential clients to know what you're advertising without having to get uncomfortably close to you!

    I strongly recommend that you keep a few extra shirts in your truck. If you are out working and are hot and sweaty, it never fails. That's when a new potential client will call you and need you to run by in about an hour to give an estimate! With a clean company shirt on hand, you are ready to make a great first impression any time. Also, any time you are putting out flyers, door hangers, etc. be sure to wear your shirts!

    We have a local screen printer that does ours at a

cost of about $5.00 per shirt. You can get them a little cheaper, but we prefer really good quality shirts.

For resources on this topic, please visit:
www.LawnBusinessResources.com

Ways of Advertising Your Competition Probably Hasn't Thought Of...

Be creative. You don't know if an advertising method will work unless you try it. A couple of the things we have tried I went into almost <u>knowing</u> they wouldn't work—but tried them anyway. We kept an open mind, though, and made some good money from some of them. Here are a few things that I haven't seen too many other lawn businesses do but they really paid off for us:

<u>Sponsor a hole on a local golf tournament</u>.
We've done this twice with good results both times. For the sponsorship, we got a sign at the hole and listings on all of the promotional materials, etc. We were also at the tournament in golf shirts with our company logo embroidered on them. People not only saw our signs at the hole we sponsored, but they also saw us! Both times we did this we got new business as a direct result.

<u>Sponsor a show or time on NPR (National Public Radio)</u>.
Don't laugh. You might want to give this a try! Depending on where you live, this can be a great way to get new clients—and 99% of the time they will be upper income clients. NPR doesn't offer ad slots like

regular radio stations, but you can "sponsor" a show or particular time and they will mention your business. We seem to have the best luck when we sponsor in the mornings or for special shows.

Hand out miniature pumpkins around Halloween!
A friend of mine who is a kindergarten teacher had some of these small pumpkins and showed them to me (miniature pumpkins are about the size of a large grapefruit). We came up with an idea to use these for advertising. We bought about 100 of the mini pumpkins and drilled a hole through the stem of each. We punched a hole in our business card, then attached the business card with some brown cord. It looked really neat and a lot of people talked about them!

Be interviewed by your local newspaper.
Almost all newspapers do business interviews for the business section. See if they would do you one for you.
They will be more likely to do one if you are offering a new service or doing something unique.
Maybe you are going to be the first in your area to offer aeration... Be sure and let the newspaper know and maybe they will do a write up on you!

Have the message in fortune cookies custom printed.

This may seem strange, but it can work! I had a friend in the window cleaning business who had these printed with the saying "Your future can look bright, why don't you call..." and the name of his window cleaning service. He attached the fortune cookie (in the wrapper) to a full color postcard and left them at potential customers' homes. He told me he received more calls from this than anything he had ever tried! People were very curious as to why they got a fortune cookie attached to a postcard at their house. He had people that didn't even use his service to call and say that was the most creative advertising they had ever received advertising a business! If you get a box or two of the fortune cookies printed, the cost per unit is not that bad.

For resources on this topic, please visit:
www.LawnBusinessResources.com

Send your business card or flyer along with another company's invoice.

You can send your flyer or business card in the envelope with another business's bill. If you are looking to work in certain areas, see who is already working in the area (a pest control company, pool services, etc.). I have not run into a business who wouldn't work with you on this. Think about it—you are basically paying them to send mail to someone they were already going to send a bill to. This is generally a mutually beneficial agreement—the other company makes money, and you get your ad out. The effectiveness is pretty high on this, too. The customer will open and read it because it is in a bill they were expecting.

Be Creative!
If you have ideas for a way of advertising, give it a try. Who knows...it just may work!

Setting Up a Referral Program or System

I think this is so important I am dedicating a couple of pages to it. Before I get started on referrals, I want to be clear. Putting out door hangers is great. Mailing postcards to the neighborhoods you want to work in produces results as well. But if you set up a good referral system, it can basically run by itself.

Have you ever thought about it? How do you find out about businesses? Where do you get your most trusted information about new services? Most of the time, you find out about these things by word of mouth or referrals. I would venture to say once you've been in business for a year or so, 90% or more of all your work will come in the form of referrals and/or word of mouth.

Here are a few ways you can go about setting up your referral system:

• Use a postcard mailing to give your existing clients an easy way to tell people about your business. You do this by sending your existing clients 10 or so postcards with stamps already on them (but not addressed to anyone). Include a letter that outlines the benefit for them. For example, they mail these to their friends, family, etc. For each new client you get from their list, they will get a free mow (or some other pre-determined item of value). How will you know where the new client came from? Simple. Put a two or three digit code that represents each of your clients on the postcards so you will know who mailed the postcard. Each time you get a phone call from a prospective client, ask how they heard about you. If they say they received a post card, ask for the code or the sender's name.

• Give them their lawn care FREE. If someone refers 10 new contracts (or however many you feel is appropriate) who become yearly customers of yours, give them their basic lawn service at no cost.

How can you afford to do this? Easy. According to the scenario we discussed earlier in the book, an average customer may be worth $1,800 per year to you. This means 10 new yearly customers are worth about $18,000 or so. If you got $18,000 worth of business referred from someone, don't you think you can afford to give them their $1,800 service? Don't you think they would be motivated to try and get the number of people needed so they can get their service free? I know they will!

• Give them a gift certificate if they refer someone. I mentioned this in another section, but it bears repeating. Let's say someone refers a new customer to you. That new customer stays and becomes a regular customer. That's worth quite a bit of money to you over the long run. Make sure the person who referred the new customer feels appreciated by giving them something! You will be the first person they think of the next time they are ready to refer someone for lawn care services.

Notes:

Chapter Three:

Customers

"If you do build a great experience, customers tell each other about that. Word of mouth is very powerful."

-Jeff Bezos

What Kind of Accounts Do You Want?

I suggest starting with residential customers and working your way up. The next section in this chapter addresses moving from residential to commercial customers.

In lawn care, you can go after several different types of properties.

- Residential
- Large Residential Properties (over an acre)
- Small Commercial Properties
- Commercial/Industrial/Office Parks
- Apartment Complexes
- Condominiums
- Municipal Properties (City / County Owned)
- Malls, shopping centers

I will touch on each of these and give you my thoughts.

Residential

This is probably the easiest and fastest type of property to get started with. They are profitable (if bid correctly). They take a relatively small amount of time and are relatively easy to do. Residential customers have huge potential for add-on services such as planting flowers, adding mulch, etc.

I personally like smaller residential properties. If you can find an area where there are a lot of homes with smaller lots and they are close together, you have found a gold mine in most cases.

One overlooked market is in homes that are for sale and are empty. Contact the realty company or property owner to find out who is maintaining the lawn for them. If you contact the realty company, you might be able to get in the owner's good graces by offering to do his office or residence FREE if he will refer his clients to you. You can build a large, profitable market share by doing this.

Large Residential Properties (over an acre)

When dealing with large properties, I prefer to get in, do my work, and get out. Larger properties are not my favorite types to work. Don't get me wrong, I'm not saying they cannot be profitable. If you are set up to do larger properties (by this I mean you have 72" cut mowers, etc.), then by all means you can make money on them.

Larger properties do generally take more time to maintain, and to do it properly you will need larger equipment and possibly a larger crew.

The problem that I run into is this: people don't seem to mind paying me $35-$55 dollars for a smaller property. Some do seem to mind writing me a check for over $100+ per visit on a larger property. When I have done larger properties like this, it also usually involved other services such as pruning a lot of smaller trees, trimming along a fence line, etc.

Small Commercial Properties

This is a great way to get started on building the commercial side of your business. You can begin with lawyers' and doctors' offices, small family-owned restaurants, etc. Use these to work your way into larger commercial accounts!

Commercial/Industrial/Office Parks

Depending on what type of property and where you are, this type of property can be very profitable. Generally, these accounts don't just want you to mow. They like to have the flowers changed out, mulch freshened up, etc. Keep in mind that the margins are not what they are for residential accounts, but the average bill is larger.

Apartment Complexes

Apartments can be a source of good income. I generally prefer for them to be mixed in with other properties, though. I don't suggest putting all of your eggs in one basket by getting 90% of your income from just a couple of apartment complexes.

Most of the time, you will have to submit a bid or proposal to either the property management company or the owner of the complex. Some apartment complexes can be as simple to do as residential accounts, or they can be more involved if you are dealing with a large complex that wants you to do everything for them (i.e. - fertilize, change out seasonal flowers, etc.).

Condominiums

My experience with condominiums is that they are looking for the cheap way out when it comes to lawn maintenance. This may not be the case in all areas, but it was certainly my experience. They pay for lawn services out of monthly dues they collect from property owners, so any money they save is more to spend on their "pet" projects. Several condominiums in our area have gone to having an in-house crew do all of their lawn care work, so it makes these jobs hard to find.

Municipal Properties

I thought I would mention municipal properties, but in many areas a town will have their own equipment and crews. I have seen a few towns that had all the latest and greatest lawn equipment (along with very nice trucks to haul them around in). If you do find a town that outsources their landscaping, be sure you follow all of their bid guidelines, etc. properly or you will not be considered for the job.

Malls/Shopping Centers

Speaking personally, the only time I have made good money on malls or shopping centers was by doing small shopping centers. The larger properties were generally much more hassle with only slightly more pay. Be sure to weigh what it's worth to you!

I also generally avoid grocery stores altogether. They often seem to blur the line between lawn care and lot maintenance, and they expect you to get up trash and debris from their lot in addition to maintaining the lawns. Be prepared for this by clarifying expectations up front if you are pursuing one of these jobs.

Getting Your First Customers

Remember, you have to start somewhere. All you need is one customer to get started, right?

Getting that first customer is the best feeling in the world! How are you going to do it? Think about your existing resources. Have you asked family and friends? How about any older relatives you have? Are they are paying someone to do their lawn? What about where you work? Who does the lawn there? How about the owner (if you work for a small business)—who does his or her lawn? Have you handed out business cards to people you meet and the people you already know? Are you bringing them to your kids' soccer games or dance recitals? Are you leaving business cards at restaurants when you go out to eat?

Set yourself a goal (like I talked about in Chapter One) to talk to 5 new potential customers each day. If you will do this day-in and day-out you will get work— probably more than you can take on. It is simply a numbers game. Talk to enough people and you are guaranteed to find people who need their lawns maintained.

I often wonder what people are doing who tell me they can't find any customers. Almost all the hard-working guys I know in the lawn industry have to turn away work. If you are aggressive in your marketing and will talk with people it won't be long until you will have more than you can do, as well.

Moving From Residential to Commercial Customers

Once you have a few residential accounts, it may be time to look at getting some commercial accounts. Don't get overwhelmed by this. It's easy to do if you take it in small steps.

Start with one small commercial customer. One is all it takes... Banks, restaurants and small retail sites are usually the easiest to get. Family-owned businesses also seem to be easier than big, corporate-owned businesses.

When starting out, try to find a property that is less than one acre. This will be an easy adjustment and will help make you look like a seasoned professional. It won't be much different than the residential customers you are already servicing.

The following are ideas to help get your foot in the door:

Friends and Relatives - Everyone works somewhere! Ask your friends and relatives who does the lawn where they work. You may get them to approach the boss (If they work at a small business) and help you find out if he or she is accepting bids.

Current Residential Customers - Do any of your current customers own a small business? I bet at least a few do. Ask if they would be willing to accept a bid. You may even want to cut them a deal if they allow you to service both.

Once you have started doing work for one commercial customer, ask them if they are happy with your work. If they are (they should be if you're doing your job!), see if you can use them as a reference for other bids. Keep repeating this process to build your references and reputation.

When you have a portfolio full of these smaller properties you can start looking at apartment complexes, large shopping centers, large manufacturing plants, and more (see the next section on how to bid on these larger properties).

*One quick note: you will need to know how or partner with people who can do sprinklers, fertilization, etc. Larger commercial customers will want a full-service company. They like for one company to take care of all of their lawn care and landscape management needs. Be sure you have these resources or can contract them out prior to approaching larger jobs.

How to Estimate for Larger Properties

When I first got started, bigger properties intimidated me. You may be used to bidding on small lawns and maybe even small commercial properties, but when it comes to large properties you may feel lost. When I went through this, I talked with several friends in the business and finally a lawn business owner in another state. He told me how he did it successfully, and it has worked wonders for me. When you look at it as one big property, it can be overwhelming. All of the mowing, all of the trimming, all of the mulch you will have to freshen up.

How in the world are you going to figure all of that??? As it turns out, my problem was that I was trying to make it too complicated. It's not hard once you know what to do.

How do you do it? He called it "chunking it down." You already know how to bid on smaller properties. Simply break the large property into smaller sections, estimate the time it will take you to do the small sections, and then add it all up.

Let's look at an apartment complex as an example. Say you have to estimate an apartment complex that has 14 buildings, a common pool area, and a leasing office. If you look at each building and know it's going to take you 20 minutes to mow each one, 5 minutes to trim, and 10 minutes to blow off the walkways, you have a pretty good idea of what it will take you to do the entire property. Once you do a couple you will be as comfortable estimating large properties as you are the small ones.

Notes:

Chapter Four:

Mowing

"Efficiency is doing things right. Effectiveness is doing the right thing."

-Zig Ziglar

Climate Zones

Most plants, grasses, etc. can be divided up by the zones in which they grow. I put this section in here because you need to know in what zone you live and what plants, grasses, etc thrive there. Get familiar with your zone and learn as much as you can about what grows in your area.

Hardiness Zones – Details

Hardiness Zones

Zone	Avg. Annual Low
2	-40° through -50°
3	-30° through -40°
4	-20° through -30°
5	-10° through -20°
6	0° through -10°
7	10° through 0°
8	20° through 10°
9	30° through 20°
10	40° through 30°

Zones 2-10 in the map have been subdivided into light- and dark-colored sections (a and b) that represent 5 F (2.8 C) differences within the 10 F (5.6 C) zone. The light color of each zone represents the colder section; the dark color, the warmer section. Zone 11 represents any area where the average annual minimum temperature is above 40 F (4.4 C).

The map shows 20 latitude and longitude lines. Areas above an arbitrary elevation are traditionally considered unsuitable for plant cropping and do not bear appropriate zone designations. There are also island zones that, because of elevation differences, are warmer or cooler than the surrounding areas and are given a different zone designation.

Note that many large urban areas carry a warmer zone designation than the surrounding countryside. The map-contains as much detail as possible, considering the vast amount of data on which it is based and its size.

Different Types of Grass

Grass Types, Mower Blades, and Mowing Height

Below is a brief summary of a few types of common grasses. You can find out more by talking to local suppliers and inquiring about what is most used in your area and why.

Bentgrass, Colonial

Bentgrass, Colonial is a fine, textured grass with few creeping stems and rhizomes. It forms a dense turf when heavily seeded and closely cropped. Used chiefly in high quality lawns and putting greens, it is more expensive to maintain than ordinary lawn grasses and is popular in cool, damp areas like New England, Oregon, and Washington. It requires fertile soil and frequent feeding. It is disease prone and must be mowed below approximately 3/4" or it becomes fluffy and forms an undesirable spongy mat. Of the several strains sold, Highland is hardiest. Astoria is bright green compared to Highland's bluish-green, but Astoria is not as drought resistant or as aggressive as Highland. Astoria, if well-managed, gives a better lawn appearance than Highland.

Kentucky Bluegrass

This is the most widely used lawn grass in the United States. Where there is adequate irrigation for it,

Kentucky Bluegrass is a hardy, long-lived, sod-forming grass that spreads by heavy underground rootstocks. Common Kentucky bluegrass will not tolerate poor drainage or high acidity, but prefers heavy, well-drained soils of good fertility that are neutral or near-neutral. It is highly drought resistant and can go into a semi-dormant condition in hot summer weather. It can be injured if mowed shorter than 1 1/2" inches, and will not tolerate heavy shade. Because it is slow to establish itself, it is often planted with faster growing "nurse" grasses that provide cover and prevent weed invasion.

Red Fescue and Chewings Fescue

These grasses rate with Kentucky Bluegrass as the most popular lawn grasses in the cool, humid regions of the United States. Red fescue spreads slowly by rhizomes. Chewings fescue is a bunch-type grower. Both are established by seeding. They are used extensively in lawn seed mixtures, grow well in shade, and tolerate high acidity. They require good drainage but will flourish in poor arid soils. Red fescue and Chewings fescue are fine textured with tough bristle-like leaves. When seeded heavily they form a dense sod that resists wear. They heal slowly when injured by insects or disease. Consistent mowing below 1 1/2" can severely damage these grasses. Improved strains of red fescue include Pennlawn, Illahee, and Rainier.

Rough Bluegrass

Rough bluegrass is a shade tolerant perennial that is easily injured by hot dry weather but is useful in lawns in the extreme northern United States. It is established by seeding. Leaves, which are the same texture as those of Kentucky bluegrass, lie flat giving the turf a glassy appearance. Rough bluegrass is lighter green than Kentucky bluegrass, and it spreads by short stolons. Its shallow root system limits its use to shady areas where traffic is light.

Ryegrass

Annual ryegrass and perennial ryegrass are propagated entirely by seed that is produced in the Pacific Northwest or imported. Much of the ryegrass in seeded lawns is a mixture of annual and perennial varieties. Many commercial lawn seed mixtures contain too much ryegrass which competes with the permanent grass seedlings for moisture and nutrients. Sometimes, however, it is advisable to include a small amount of ryegrass in lawn seed mixtures on slopes in order to help prevent soil erosion. Coarse clumps of ryegrass may persist for years. It often results in ragged looking lawns that are difficult to mow. It is a very wet grass to cut. In the southern United States annual (common) ryegrass is used for winter over-seeding of Bermuda grass in lawns and on golf greens and tees. This allows southern lawns to stay green year-round.

Tall Fescue

Tall fescue is tall-growing bunch grass with coarse, dense leaves and a strong root system. It is established by seeding. It is also used for pasture grasses. Tolerant of moderate shade, it grows in wet, dry, acidic, or

alkaline soils but prefers well-drained fertile soils.
Because of their wear resistant qualities, two highly
drought-resistant strains of tall fescue, Kentucky 31
fescue and Alta fescue, are often used on playgrounds,
athletic fields, service yards, and the like.

Bermuda Grass

Bermuda grass grows vigorously and can become a
tenacious pest in other cultivated garden areas. It
dislikes shade, poor drainage, high acidity, or low
fertility. It needs heavy applications of readily available
nitrogen. Although drought resistant, it requires
moderate amounts of water during dry periods and must
be clipped closely in order to form a dense turf.

Each variety of Bermuda grass has a fairly
specialized use. Common Bermuda, a coarse grass, is
the only variety for which seed is available. Other
varieties are established vegetatively. Common lawn
varieties include Tiflawn, Everglades No. 1, Ormond,
Sunturf, and Texturf 10. Tiflawn is finer textured than
common Bermuda grass and is greener. Ormond is
coarser and grows more upright than Everglades No. 1.
Of the three varieties, Everglades No. 1 requires the
least maintenance.

Bermuda grass varieties used in high quality lawns
and in golf course putting greens and fairways include
Tifgreen, Tiffine, Tifway, Bayshore, and Tifdwarf. These
are medium green and fine textured varieties.

Carpet Grass

This is a rapidly spreading stoloniferous perennial

that produces a dense, compact turf under mowing but is very coarse textured. It can be established most cheaply by seeding, or quickly by sprigging or sodding. It grows best in moist, sandy-loam soils or those with fairly high moisture content year around. Carpet grass does poorly in dry soils or in arid regions. It thrives with limited fertilization in poor soils but is very sensitive to lack of iron. Although resistant to trampling, heavy wear, disease, and insects, it will not tolerate salt-water spray. It must be mowed fairly frequently.

Centipede Grass

Centipede grass spreads rapidly by short creeping stems that form new plants at each node, forming a dense, vigorous turf that is highly resistant to weed invasion. It is usually established vegetatively, but some seed is available. It is considered the best low-maintenance lawn in the southern part of the United States, but can be severely damaged by salt water spray and lack of iron. An annual application of a complete fertilizer will improve its quality. Although drought resistant, it should be watered during extremely dry periods. It is very low in nutritional value and should not be planted near pastures.

St. Augustine Grass

St. Augustine grass is a creeping perennial that spreads by long stolons that produce short, leafy branches. This is the number one shade grass in the southernmost United States. It grows successfully south of Augusta, Georgia, westward to the coastal regions of

Texas. Seed is unavailable; it is established vegetatively. It will withstand salt water spray, and grows best in fertile, moist soils. It produces good turf in the muck soils of Florida, but liberal applications of high-nitrogen fertilizer are necessary, especially in sandy soils. It can be seriously damaged by diseases and insects.

Zoysia Japonica

This is a low growing perennial that spreads by stolons and shallow root stocks. This grass forms a dense weed-, disease-, and insect-resistant turf. It grows best in a region south of a line from Philadelphia to San Francisco. Above that line the shorter growing season makes it impractical. It turns straw colored with the first frost and remains off- color until warm spring weather revives it.

Common zoysia japonica is coarse textured and excellent for large areas like airfields and playgrounds; however Meyer zoysia is desirable for home lawns. Meyer is more vigorous, keeps its color later in the fall and regains it earlier in the spring. There is no seed, but the sod is available from nurseries. It will survive in low-fertility soils but responds well to liberal applications of fertilizers with a high nitrogen content. Emerald zoysia, a dense, dark green hybrid between zoysia japonica and mascarene grass seems superior to Meyer zoysia in the southern U.S.

Fertilizers

Fertilizers and Their Application

I'm just going to give you the basics on fertilization. I highly encourage you to talk with your local wholesale supplier of fertilizers and learn all you can. This is a big money maker and is not generally hard work at all. In the beginning I would suggest sticking to granule fertilizers instead of liquid.

People who buy my guide range from the Southeast where we are to Florida, California, Texas, New Jersey and everywhere in between. Again, to find out what works best for your area, I suggest talking to your local wholesale supplier or other fertilizer experts. They can tell you what works and what other lawn care companies are buying. Some suppliers even have special mixes they will suggest to you for your area, the types of grass you are working on and the time of year.

Fertilizers contain nutrients that plants and grass need to grow. A typical fertilizer contains:
N (nitrogen),
P (phosphorus), and
K (potassium), listed in that order.

Below is an explanation of the three numbers in a fertilizer analysis. A 5-10-15 fertilizer, for example, contains 5% nitrogen, 10% phosphorus, and 15%

potassium.

Nitrogen (N), the first number that you see on a bag of fertilizer, is primarily responsible for plant growth and color. Nitrogen is what makes the grass greener, so to speak. Adding nitrogen to plants has the most visible effect on them. Too little of it causes yellowish leaves and weak roots. Too much nitrogen can make a plant over-succulent, dull, and soft because of thinner cell walls. This makes it susceptible to cold, drought, disease, and pests. Plants lose nitrogen to competition by weeds, use by microorganisms, leaching, and volatilizing. Nitrogen comes in organic, synthetic, and "synthetic organic" formulas. It's the cheapest plant nutrient, and buying combined fertilizers by the amount of nitrogen in them permits tailoring soil enrichment to specific plant needs. It also means a better price for the customer and a better profit for you. As a final note, be sure and get slow release nitrogen. This provides the most benefit for the lawn over time and results in happier customers!

Phosphorus (P), the middle number on the bag and an important part of DNA, RNA, and some enzymes, assists the plant's energy system and respiration, and plants can store it for later use. It shows up naturally in some soil minerals, and inorganic and organic compounds.

Potassium (K), the last number on the bag and the third major plant nutrient, doesn't become part of the plant but regulates the plant's life processes. Potassium is a catalyst for water intake, transpiration, and enzyme actions. Plants need it to form and transfer starches, sugars, and oils. Potassium increases plant vigor and disease resistance. Most soils contain potassium but it is usually unavailable and is best added before planting and regularly after that. Adding too much potassium, however, can cause a magnesium deficiency, especially in sandy soils.

Below is an example of a couple types of fertilizer and how you may use them.

15-0-15
This is a General-purpose landscape fertilizer for shrubs, small trees, lawns, flowers, and groundcovers. As a general rule, select one with 7.5% slow-release nitrogen.

15-5-15
This would be appropriate for new plantings, where the available phosphorus may help establishment. It is also for short-term plantings such as flowering annuals or for when a soil test indicates a need for phosphorus. Again, select one with 7.5% slow-release nitrogen.

Note: Keep in mind that too much Nitrogen will burn up a lawn—even in granule form. Don't overdo it!

How High to Mow

I like to cut the grass a little high. Why? First of all, it's better for the grass. Second, it looks better! Here are a few quick references on mow height for different regions and varieties.

Arid Region Grasses
Blue Grama: 2 to 3"
Buffalo: 2 to 3"

Cool Season Grasses
Bentgrass, Colonial: 2 to 3"
Kentucky Bluegrass: 2 to 2 1/2" (Mow higher during summer dormancy)
Red Fescue: 2-3"
Rough Bluegrass: 2 to 2 1/2"
Ryegrass: 2 to 3"
Tall Fescue: 2"

Warm Season Grasses
Bermuda: 2 to 3 1/2" (I prefer to cut this a little higher)
Carpet Grass: 2 to 2 1/2"
Centipede Grass: 2 to 2 1/2"
St. Augustine Grass: 2 to 2 1/2"
Zoysia Grass: 2 to 2 1/2"

Mower Blades and Sharpening

Blade Sharpening

If you notice that you are having a thin line of uncut grass being left as you mow or your blades just don't seem to be cutting good anymore, they may need to be sharpened. Sharpening can be done with a hand file, electric grinder, or a specialized sharpener.

Blades are generally sharpened at a 30-degree angle (the amount of sharpening will depend on the usage involved). If you aren't sure, try to follow the previous angle on the blade. For nicks and gouges, you may have to take off a considerable amount of metal to get the nick or gouge out.

> For resources on this topic, please visit:
> www.LawnBusinessResources.com

Blade Balancing

If you are experiencing a vibration coming from the mower deck that you didn't notice previously, chances are you have a blade out of balance. An out-of-balance blade can cause damage to the deck pulleys and/or crankshaft. A blade balancer is the best bet to get a good balance (Magna Matic makes these as well).

If you put a nail through the center of the hole of the blade and position the blade level with the ground you will see if the blade is off-center. If the blade remains level it is balanced, if it weights down on one side it needs adjustment. To fix this just grind down the heavier part of the blade until it balances.

Lawn Striping

Lawn striping is very cool and generally impresses your customers—and makes their neighbors jealous! You can make a lawn look very impressive using this technique.

Striping is pretty simple, yet looks very impressive. To stripe, you will need a striping or roller kit. You can get striping kits from some of the lawn mower manufacturers, or you can order them online. Then all you need to do is mow in opposite directions on each pass. The striping kit will do the rest of the work. Be careful not to make weird turns or passes, as it will show up in your patterns. You want to run all the way to the end of the property then make your turns.

Once you do a couple of lawns with your striping, take good quality pictures of the lawns. You can use the pictures on your advertising. Also, you can bet people will ask the homeowner who does the lawn (Use this as another reminder to leave business cards with your clients!).

*Note: Striping works best with cool season grasses (Rye, etc.). It will work on other grasses, but it seems to show up better in grasses with high moisture content.

For resources on this topic, please visit:
www.LawnBusinessResources.com

Bagging or Mulching

99% of the work we do is simply mowing. You can get a mulching kit for just about any mower these days, but they will slow down your mowing. If someone wants us to bag their lawn, we charge them extra (I usually charge about $10 extra, depending on the size of the lawn). I do this because, not only does it slow me down but I have to pay to dispose of the clippings. I just can't afford to do it free.

There are special mowers that are made just for finer lawns where the customer wants the clippings bagged. One mower that I will note is made by "Walker". As you can see in the picture below, it is set up to bag and does a really nice job. Walker mowers also do a great job of getting up leaves in the fall.

How to Estimate and What to Charge

Estimating and knowing what to charge your customers is not that complicated to figure out. I'll give you my crash course in both!

Find out your area's rates
If you aren't sure what the going rates are in your area, you can do a couple of things:

1. You can talk to your competitors.
Find out what they are charging their clients. If they won't discuss this openly with you, get them to bid on mowing your lawn or have a friend call them.

2. You can ask at your local mower service center. Most likely they will know what the going rates are for your area.

3. Ask potential clients what they are currently paying. Most people love to talk and will gladly tell you what they are paying for their lawn service. Keep in mind, too, that 99% of clients don't swap solely because of price. They swap because the people doing their lawn started doing a bad job or didn't service it as often as they wanted them to. Don't fall into this trap and lose customers!

Have a minimum charge
I would suggest you set a minimum price and stick to it. I have a minimum charge of $35, and I won't mow for less than that. I'm not saying your charge has to be $35, but you should have some sort of minimum. It's simply not worth my time to unload for anything less than that. If you mow for less in that same time you could

be mowing another property that is worth a lot more to you (I discussed this previously in Chapter One)!

<u>Estimating 101</u>
There are two easy ways to estimate. Please don't make this harder than it is!

Estimating by time:

I prefer to use this method. It has served me well and is not too complicated. To estimate, figure how long it will take you to mow the property. You can do this by visualizing actually mowing it. Before long, you will be able to look at a property and tell how long it will take you. Multiply your estimated work time by $1 per minute. If it is going to take you 45 minutes to mow, you would charge $40 to $45 (the dollar figure you multiply by may change based on the going rate in your area).

Estimating by square footage:

You can also measure a lawn with a measuring wheel and then multiply that amount by a certain amount per sq ft. This is a decent way to estimate, but what if it takes me longer to do 20,000 sq ft in one place than it does in another? Keep this in mind if you choose this method of estimation.

<u>Here are some helpful tips and ways to figure spaces:</u>
To get square footage of a lawn:
Multiply the length by the width.
Example: A lawn 500 ft wide by 400 feet deep would be 20,000 square feet.

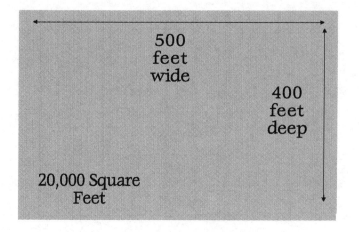

No matter which method you choose, it is not hard to get very proficient at estimating. It won't take you long until you can look at a property and easily tell what you will need to charge to mow it and make a profit.

Submitting a Proposal to Customers

 This is another aspect of the lawn business that you shouldn't sweat over. Do a good job on it, but don't worry for days about submitting a proposal for the lawn care maintenance for a homeowner or business.

I would suggest submitting a proposal with a good cover letter. They should detail what you are proposing to do, the frequency of your visits, and a breakdown of the cost. On the next few pages are examples of what a basic cover letter and proposal should look like (and what information it should include).

For downloadable copies of these documents, please visit:
www.LawnBusinessResources.com

Dave's Quick Cuts
1234 Main Street
Gadsden, Alabama 54112
Phone: 256-852-7412
Fax: 256-852-1236
dave@davesquickcuts.com

Ms. Mary Johnson
654 Oak Street
Trussville, AL 35126
08/08/2008
RE: Lawn Care Proposal

Dear Ms. Johnson,

Thank you for the opportunity for Dave's Quick Cuts to submit the attached proposal for lawn care needs. This proposal will ensure all of your lawn care needs will be met in a timely and professional manner.

Dave's Quick Cuts has been serving clients in the Trussville area since 1995. We work hard to maintain professional, affordable, and dependable lawn services. I will be glad to meet with you personally to discuss this proposal.

If I can answer any of your questions or can assist you in any way in determining your landscape maintenance needs, please let me know. You can reach me any time at our office by calling 256-852-7412.

Respectfully,

Dave
Dave's QuickCuts

Dave's QuickCuts
1234 Main Street
Gadsden, Alabama 54112
Phone: 256-852-7412
Fax: 256-852-1236
dave@davesquickcuts.com

Ms. Mary Johnson
654 Oak Street
Trussville, Al 35126
08/08/2008

Lawn Care and Landscape Management Proposal
Property: _____
Address: _____
City/State/Zip: _____
Date:_____
Contact: _____

Dave's Quick Cuts is providing the following lawn care
and landscape maintenance proposal for Bob Smith for
the _____ season.
If you have any questions, please feel free to contact us
at our office at the number above.

LAWN CARE AND GROUNDS MAINTENANCE
PROPOSAL

Turf Mowing / Trimming:
Cost $ _____
All turf areas will be mowed _____ times during the
mowing season.
Height of cut will depend on species and local

conditions. If it rains heavily or we experience extended dry periods, we may mow more or less than usual.
With each mowing, we will trim around all buildings, and other obstacles within the area.
All debris will be removed from the grass areas prior to mowing. Excess grass clippings will be raked or bagged as needed to maintain a neat appearance.

1. Weed Control: Cost $ _____
We will maintain all flowerbeds, ornamental mulch beds and tree rings to make sure they are weed free.
This may be done by hand or by using herbicides.

2. Edging: Cost $ _____
All sidewalks, driveways, and curbs will be edged to maintain a neat appearance.

3. Sidewalk Weeds: Cost $ _____
All seams and cracks in sidewalks and curbs will be kept weed free.

4. Pruning: Cost $ _____
All ornamental shrubs, bushes, etc will be pruned _____ times during the mowing season to ensure a professionally maintained appearance.

MULCHING
1. Initial Mulch: Cost $ _____
This will be placing of mulch in areas where mulch is not present or is s deteriorated it needs to be replaced.
Mulch layer shall not exceed 3-4 inches in depth.

2. Top Dress Mulch: Cost $ _____

Areas that were mulched will get a new layer of mulch. Total depth of top dress mulch will be about two (2) inches.

3. Mulch Bed Edging: Cost $_____
Mulch beds, shrub beds, flower beds, and tree rings will have a sharp, well- defined edge made by hand or using a mechanical edger.

LEAF REMOVAL AND PROPERTY CLEAN-UP
1. Leaf Removal: Cost $_____
Also known as fall leaf clean up. All leaves will be removed from the turf areas, and mulch bed areas_____ times per mowing season (usually in the fall).

2. Spring Clean-Up: Cost $_____
All leaves and miscellaneous debris will be collected and removed from the entire property as part of the spring clean-up.

TOTAL ANNUAL COST $_____

*PLEASE NOTE WE OFFER MONTHLY BILLING:
This breaks up the cost of our services to make them as affordable as possible. If you chose monthly billing the bill for the above services would be _____ per month for months.

Yearly Contracts

It is not necessary to have people sign a yearly contract. Some people will be turned off by this even though others wouldn't mind. One good thing about a contract is that you can explain to the customer that you use the contract in order to break up the cost of their lawn care services over a 12 month period. It evens out the cost of your services and makes it more affordable. You can include the cost of mowing, fall leaf removal, mulching, etc. There is a sample contract on the next few pages.

LawnPro business software has a contract section built in. It prints a contract for you with your customer's information filled in and will even divide the billing into 12 (or however many you want) equal installments.

For a downloadable copy of this document, please visit:
www.LawnBusinessResources.com

Things To Remember

1. _____
2. _____
3. _____
4. _____
5. _____
6. _____
7. _____
8. _____
9. _____
10. _____

**PSP Financial Home Mortgage
&
Commercial Loan Corporation**
9093 Ridgefield Drive, Suite 204
Frederick, MD 21701
301-698-0828 / 877-698-0828
www.frederickhomefinder.com

Dave's Quick Cuts
1234 Main Street
Gadsden, Alabama 54112
Phone: 256-852-7412
Fax: 256-852-1236
dave@davesquickcuts.com

Mr. Bob Smith
654 Oak Street
Vancouver, BC V7K 8F3
06/18/2008

LAWN CARE CONTRACT This contract is
effective as of:

This lawn care service contract is between Dave's Quick
Cuts, located at 1234 Main Street, which will be referred
to as "Dave's Quick Cuts", and Mr. Bob Smith who is
referred to as "Owner" in this contract.

1. Dave's Quick Cuts will service the lawn of the Owner
approximately _____ times during the lawn service
year .
Services will begin on _____ and continue
through _____ .

A service can include, but isn't limited to: grass cutting,
trimming, edging of driveway and sidewalks, grass
removal from sidewalks and driveway.
Complete fall leaf clean-up can be completed for an
additional cost of $_____ and will be billed
separate.

103

Any additional services will be billed separate and written up in a separate agreement or addendum to this contract.
(Such as clean up after a storm, planting flowers, putting in mulch, clean-up of leaves out of flower beds but only in the lawn, etc.)
Owner will pay $_____ per month for_____ consecutive months.
The service will be billed on or about the 1st of each month and is due and payable by the 15th of the same month.
Either party may cancel this contract with thirty (30) days written notice mailed to the party at the addresses listed in this contract. During this thirty (30) day period, lawn service will continue at the normal rates agreed upon under this contract.

Upon cancellation any money due for services performed up and until that date shall be due within 10 days of the final visit for services made by Dave's Quick Cuts.

The term of this contract will be on-going from year to year. If there is any change in the service fees from year to year you will be notified in writing 30 days before the date of such increase.

The billing period of this contract shall be through of each year after the first year.

Any amounts past due under this contract will be charged one and one half percent (1.5%) per month for anything past due over thirty (30) days. This amount will be added to the amount normally due under this contract. Once you are past due 30 days or more we reserve the right to stop service.

This contract along with the addendum (if attached and signed) constitutes the full and complete agreement between the parties hereto.

Dave's Quick Cuts

_____

HOMEOWNER/ PROPERTY OWNER

_____

Date _____

Are You Mowing In Circles?

Mowing in circles is a huge time killer and something I see a lot of people new to the business doing. When you mow a lawn, the fastest way to mow is to make a couple of passes around the outside of the property. Once you have mowed the perimeter, make passes back and forth across the property. This will actually speed up your mowing. Try it and time yourself both ways!

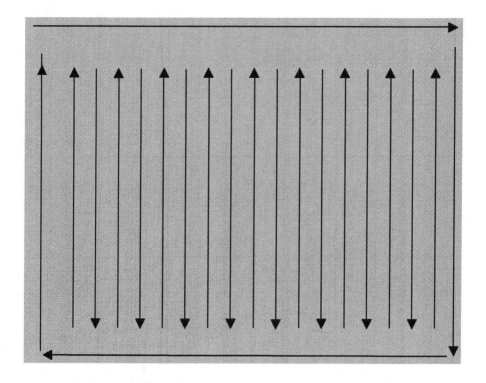

How Fast Can You Mow?

Only after you mow for a while can you get a real feel for how long it will take you to do a lawn. In the meantime, I can give some general guidelines.

Multiply your ground speed (how fast your mower will mow) by the cutting width divided by 120. The number 120 allows for an 80% efficiency rate. Wide open spaces will be a little higher, tight areas with a lot of trimming work, etc. will be a little slower. Other variables, such as wet grass, may slow you down as well.

Example: a mower with a speed of 5 mph with a cutting width of 48" would let you mow 2 acres per hour (5 mph x 48 in cut divided by 120).

Trimming

Add 25% or so to your time estimate for weed eating or trimming. If there are a lot of trees or a fence to trim, be sure to take that into account when doing your estimate.

Blowing

Blowing off the driveways and walkways adds about 5%-8% to your time. After you do this for a while you'll get a feel for pretty much the exact time it will take you.

Here's a chart breaking all if these calculations down so you don't have to figure it out each time:

80% efficiency = average mowing conditions
100% efficiency = wide open terrain

Ground Speed	36" Deck		48" Deck		52" Deck		61" Deck		72" Deck	
(MPH)	80%	100%	80%	100%	80%	100%	80%	100%	80%	100%
4	1.20	1.60	1.60	2.13	1.73	2.31	2.03	2.71	2.40	3.20
4.5	1.35	1.80	1.80	2.40	1.95	2.6	2.29	3.05	2.70	3.60
5	1.50	2.00	2.00	2.67	2.17	2.89	2.54	3.39	3.00	4.00
5.5			2.20	2.93	2.38	3.18	2.80	3.73	3.30	4.40
6			2.40	3.20	2.60	3.47	3.05	4.07	3.60	4.80
6.5			2.60	3.47	2.82	3.76	3.30	4.41	3.90	5.20
7			2.80	3.394	3.033	3.677	3.558	4.313	4.200	5.091
7.5			3.00	3.636	3.250	3.939	3.813	4.621	4.500	5.455
8			3.20	3.879	3.467	4.202	4.067	4.929	4.800	5.818
8.5			3.40	4.121	3.683	4.465	4.321	5.237	5.100	6.182
9			3.60	4.364	3.900	4.727	4.575	5.545	5.400	6.545
9.5			3.80	4.606	4.117	4.990	4.829	5.854	5.700	6.909
10					4.33	5.252	5.083	6.162	6.00	7.273

Here are a few tips:
1. Try and plan out your path so you are mowing everywhere you ride. Start mowing at the farthest point and work your way back to the truck. In other words when you are done mowing you should be just about sitting at your truck. If you have to drive back to your truck when you are done it may only take 2 minutes, but figuring that up over a month's time adds up. It will also be less wear on the grass and the mower.
2. Don't spend 5 minutes trying to fit a mower into a place it doesn't belong. I have been guilty of this. Get your helper to take care of it with the trimmer or your finish mower.
3. Use the right piece of equipment for the job. Make

sure the mower you are using is the best for the job. I have small properties where it would seem to be faster to mow with the 60" zero turn mower. If you take time to think it over, though, you can mow the property a lot faster with a 36" walk behind simply because of all the small areas you would have to go back and trim if you did it with the larger mower.

There is no magic bullet to mowing faster, but be sure to use common sense. If you save a few minutes here and a few minutes there, it really adds up over time. If you save 10 minutes a day, you have an extra hour each week to make more money!

Notes:

Chapter Five:

Equipment

"Some say opportunity knocks only once, that is not true. Opportunity knocks all the time, but you have to be ready for it. If the chance comes, you must have the equipment to take advantage of it."

-Louis L'Amour

Choosing Your Equipment

Having the right equipment is essential to your success in this business. You might be tempted to think you are saving money by using homeowner-grade equipment, but I can assure you this is not the case. It is actually costing you more money than you realize. Even if the equipment doesn't break down often (as it probably will), you're losing time (and money) because the homeowner-grade equipment cuts slower. This is not just my opinion. It's FACT. Discuss with your local lawn care dealer the types of properties you will be working on. Most dealers will let you demo their equipment. I definitely suggest that you take advantage of this and try out a mower before you buy.

The next few sections are going to show you what equipment we use and how we set everything up. This will include:

Setting Up Your Trailer
Zero Turn Radius Mowers
Walk Behind Mowers
Trim Mowers
Backpack Blowers
Stick Edgers
Line Trimmers
Hedge Trimmers
Bed Edgers
Miscellaneous Hand Tools

Setting Up Your Trailer

Before I go too far into the chapter on equipment, I want to talk about setting up your equipment trailer. When I started out, I tried mine several different ways and have now developed a system that works best for me. Some of you will want a setup exactly like I have, and some will not want certain things. Other people may want a 100% different setup. I am just going to show you what I have to give you some ideas to get started.

Setting up your trailer properly is another way to save time. Getting equipment on and off the trailer as quick as possible will make each job quicker. Save just a few minutes at each site and it really adds up over time.

Here is the way I set up my trailer:

I started with a 6' 10" x 12' Trailer. It was built by a local company who really does quality work. I had them add two things to the trailer to make my life easier:

1. A mesh box on the front to store our gas cans, trimmer string, etc.

2. Tie down hooks around the outside to make it easier to secure our mowers.

We added racks for our trimmers and edgers.

We added a rack for our leaf blower.

We added a rack for our water cooler.

We added a rack for our rakes and
shovels.

Here's the trailer with our trimmer, edger, blower, cooler,
and hand tools.

Zero Turn Radius Mowers

When I started out I was using a regular mower like the one below. It was a 17 HP, 48" cut. John Deere financed it and I paid it off in less than one full season.

As soon as I could afford to, we moved up to a zero turn radius mower (like the one at the top of the page), and I can't tell you how much quicker and better it mows! If you can possibly afford it, I would suggest going with a commercial grade zero turn radius mower from the beginning. The time you save in mowing alone will help it pay for itself in about the same amount of time.

You can get zero turn mowers from 32 inch up to 72+ inch cut. They can be liquid cooled or air cooled.

Engine sizes can be up to and even over 30 HP! Most manufacturers offer a diesel option, as well. Ideally, I would suggest a 60", liquid cooled zero turn with a 27 or 31 hp engine. If you watch your local newspaper classifieds, near the end of the season you can get some very good deals on zero turn mowers with very low hours. I have seen some sold for almost ½ of what they cost new only a few months earlier.

I will repeat this later, but when dealing with your equipment, always wear hearing and eye protection!

Walk Behind Mowers

When it comes to walk behind mowers you have a couple of choices to make. First of all, you can get a belt drive or hydrostatic drive. Hydrostatics will cost more but they are well worth it in my opinion. A hydrostatic will pull you and still cut wet grass with no problem.
In some models you won't get an electric start until you get to a certain hp motor, so watch for this if it's important to you.

A second choice deals with your motor and deck width. With walk behinds, you can get mowing decks 36" and up from most manufacturers. As for engines, I would get a minimum of a 17 HP but would prefer a 19 HP or bigger.

I know they are called walk behind mowers because you can, well, walk behind them...but I would recommend you also get a Sulky to ride on. These come in several sizes and types from a few different manufacturers.

Trim Mowers

You will need a good trim mower. You can use it for any number of things, and it's great for getting in small, tight spaces or trimming small ditches that would take too long to do with a line trimmer.

Mine has a 6 hp Briggs and Straton engine and a mulching kit (with the option to bag if you want to). It was about $350, and I have been using it for over 3 years now with no major problems at all. It is simple enough that I service it myself (changing the sparkplug, air filter, etc).

Here again, don't forget that hearing and eye protection!

Backpack Blowers

Having a good backpack blower is priceless. You can use it year round for various types of jobs. We use ours for blowing grass clippings in the summer and for getting up leaves in the fall.

The blower I use is a Husqvarna 165BT. When you buy a blower, other than the output the main thing I would look for is to make sure you like where the throttle is. With blowers you have the option to have the trigger on the tube or mounted on a handle coming out from the side of the blower. I prefer to the one that is tube mounted. This is personal preference, so be sure to go to your local dealer and check out both styles.

Stick Edgers

You absolutely have to get a stick edger as soon as you can. I wouldn't even suggest starting a lawn care business without owning one. Not only does it make your work look more professional, you can charge extra for the services (or give it away as a bonus to get a new customer, etc.).

A stick edger can make a very neat and clean edge around flower beds, driveways, walkways, etc. Most properties don't have to be edged every visit, but you can do it every other visit in most cases.

My stick edger is an Echo PE-260 bent shaft edger. I have tried straight shaft and I just prefer this style. Again, head to your local dealer and check out both. Mine isn't the top of the line or the cheapest; it's a good middle-of-the-line commercial edger.

Line Trimmers

This is where I see a lot of businesses using equipment they bought at the local "big box" stores. That's okay, but in my opinion you will get better service and longer life out of the models your local lawn care equipment dealer sells.

I tried out several good models, but ultimately settled on the Stihl 4 Mix. It is very easy to load the trimmer string, and I have not had a minute's trouble out of my trimmer.

This will be the last time I remind you of it in this chapter if you promise to listen—ALWAYS wear hearing and eye protection!

Hedge Trimmers

Depending on where you live, this is another great way to make even more money off of your existing clients. You can trim all sorts of hedges and get anywhere from $8 up per hedge. If you aren't doing this for your clients someone is! They have to either do it themselves or they are paying someone other than you. Either way, you are losing money!

You might want to practice this at your house a few times to make sure you have it down. Most people don't think lopsided bushes are very funny!

Bed Edgers

Bed edgers let you make a nice, clean edge for new or existing flower and mulch beds. You don't have to rush out and buy one of these. I rented one for the longest time and then finally decided I wanted to have one. They are great money makers (you can read more about them in Chapter Six). The company that makes the one above is www.eztrench.com.

Miscellaneous Hand Tools

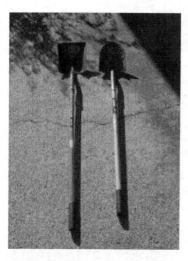

You will need an assortment of hand tools. This may include handheld trimmers, small pruners, shovels, rakes, etc. You can get good quality hand held tools at your local home improvement store. I would recommend that you buy commercial quality (fiberglass handles, etc.). They don't cost that much more and they last a good bit longer.

Another tool I like to carry is a pole saw/pruner (pictured here). Again, you can make great extra money from your existing clients by trimming the occasional low hanging branch. Remember, you can't do the job if you don't have the tools to do it with. You don't want to make a client wait on their request until you have the time to make a trip to get a shovel, pole saw, etc.

Notes:

Chapter Six:

Additional Services

"You will either step forward into growth or you will step back into safety."

-Abraham Maslow

Selling More to Customers You Already Have

It's a proven fact that it costs less to sell to you existing customers than it does to get new customers. Some surveys say it can cost as much as 5 times as much to get a new customer. With that said, why not try to get all you can from your existing clients? You can add services to what you already do and sell them to the people who already trust and use you.

There are 3 ways to get more money out of your business:

1.   Sell more to your existing clients
2.   Get more clients
3.   Sell more often to existing clients

The easiest way is to sell more to your existing customers. Let's discuss how you can do more of that.

Add on Businesses to
Make Even More Money

Most successful lawn care businesses have more work than they can do in the spring and summer months. The problem is that you want to make good money year round, right?

Once you have a customer base, you should consider adding some additional services you can offer those customers. There's no faster or easier way to increase your profits than to sell more to the people you are already working for.

Here are a few of the add on businesses you may want to consider:

- Fall Leaf Clean Up
- Snow Plowing
- Low Voltage Landscape Lighting
- Holiday Lighting
- Bed Edging
- Sprinkler Systems
- Aeration
- Dethaching
- Overseeding
- Pine Straw and Pine Mulch
- Concrete Curbing
- Hydroseeding
- Planting Seasonal Flowers

Fall Leaf Clean Up

Fall leaf clean up, like many other aspects of this business, can be done several different ways. You can blow the leaves into a pile and load them manually onto a trailer or you can use a "Leaf Loader" vacuum to load them onto a trailer. The one pictured below is made by www.giant-vac.com.

You can also use a mower with a bagging system set up just for picking up leaves.

I charge double or triple what I would get to mow to do the leaf cleanups. For instance, if I had a lawn that I charged $45 to mow I would get approximately $120 to do the leaf cleanup.

You can figure out what it will take you and a helper per hour to do the leaf clean up and then price it out as a simple quote. NEVER tell the customer you get a certain amount per hour and you think it will take you two hours.

Snow Plowing

I will have to give you secondhand information here. I have been told a lot about this, but we don't do much snow plowing in Alabama!

If you are far enough north that snow is a pest, the businesses I have spoken with tell me there is more money to be made doing this than there is in mowing.

Low Voltage Landscape Lighting

Low voltage lighting is a great add-on business. I wish we had more of these jobs to do. We've done a few low voltage landscape lighting jobs over the past year. It's easy money, it looks professional, and it makes customers happy!

We generally charge $150-$200 per light that we install. This includes the light, wiring and transformer. The price will fluctuate if the customer wants lights that are special order or are very expensive. The results of these jobs were impressive and the customers were very satisfied. As a matter of fact, one of the jobs we got was a direct referral from another lighting job we did!

Our local irrigation supplier carries several lines of low voltage landscape lighting. They gave us the basics and we went from there. To be honest, landscape lighting is not very complicated to hook up. The main thing to watch for is making sure each light is even.

Be sure and check with your local city and town governments prior to adding this service to your business. In some areas you have to have a licensed electrician do the wiring. Be sure to obey all local laws regarding offering this service.

I have a DVD on installing low voltage landscape lighting. You can find more about it at www.LawnBusinessResources.com

Holiday Lighting

I am really, really starting to like this as an add-on business. I feel like this is still a ground floor opportunity. In the next few years I think you will see more and more companies specializing strictly in low voltage and holiday lighting.

There are tons of possibilities here. You can begin putting up lights in October and do them all the way to Christmas. I start advertising in September by sending out full color postcards to existing customers. If this is your first season, you will want to buy your lights in August or so. We have seen situations where businesses couldn't get certain lights, colors, etc. when they waited until the last minute to order them.

We received a couple of calls at the last minute this year where the customer was having a party and wanted the house to look neat for the occasion. This is part of the reason you want to stock up early!

It doesn't take a ton of money to get started, and the business seems to grow more each year. We did a couple of houses the first year (one of them being mine so I could get a feel for how long it would take, etc.), but have done several more each season. At first customers won't come to you asking about this service, and you will have to market it heavily. After you complete a few jobs, though, word of mouth kicks in.

Customers really like this service for several reasons. They don't have to buy the lights and store them all year (you rent them to the customer and include it in your price). They simply call you to install and take down the lights. They don't have any of the hassle to deal with and still get to enjoy having a festive home for the holidays!

The market for this seems to be more of the middle to upper end homes. Average job tickets are from $250-$400. Profit margins are 30-60% depending on the job, etc. Don't try to skimp on equipment to raise your profit margins—I would be sure to buy quality lights. After all, you are renting them to the customer year after year, so you want lights that will last. You also don't want to receive constant calls to come back and fix lights all season!

You can get into this business a couple of ways. You can buy a franchise or you can simply go it alone.

For a list of companies to contact for more information on this topic, please visit:
www.LawnBusinessResources.com

Bed Edging

Bed edging can make a good deal of money (even if you have to rent a machine to do it!). When someone refers to this service, they generally are not talking about edging with a stick edger like you do along the driveways and walkways. There is special equipment to do this job.

Here's a simple guide to pricing this service:

New bed edges: I charge $0.60 - 1.00 per lineal foot. Be sure to push the dirt the machine generates back into the bed and then mulch over it.

Freshen up existing beds: I wouldn't charge less than $0.40 per lineal foot.

Don't give this service away. People will pay for this, so you should capitalize on it. Most people understand this is an add-on service. You can tell if they have tried to do bed edging themselves in the past. If they have, they understand that without a machine to do the work it's very hard to do and to make look good. They will gladly pay you the 1.00 a foot to have it done properly!

Sprinkler Systems

There are two ways to go about this. You can learn to do irrigation installation and repair or you can partner with someone...

When we were first getting started, we didn't do irrigation work ourselves. We partnered up with a local irrigation contractor and then would mark up his work 15-20% to the customer.

Now we do the irrigation work ourselves.

If you would like to know more about how to do irrigation, I have a DVD on this.

For supplemental information and videos on this topic, please visit:
www.LawnBusinessResources.com

Aeration

Aeration does for lawn soil what tilling does for other garden soils. It lets the soil breathe by extracting 2" to 4" plugs from the lawn 2" to 6" apart in each direction. The plugs or "cores" lay on the surface where they decompose a little before being raked away. The process is called aeration because it makes spaces in the soil for the roots to get air, water, and nutrients.

When the soil is damp you can aerate with a power aerator. Don't even think about manual aeration. The worst kind of aeration is called spiking. It does nothing more than poke holes in the soil and compact it more around the holes.

The best quality aerating is done with a machine that pulls up cores $1/2$" to $3/4$" in diameter. Good aerators cost from $2,000 to $4,000. You can rent less expensive models from rental agencies, so I suggest trying one out before adding aeration to your list of professional services.

Post-aeration fertilization, amendment, and watering encourage deeper root growth. With lots of little holes all over it, the lawn soaks up water more efficiently, too, so it's a good way to reduce water loss on slopes. The only soil that should not be aerated is a sandy one, which already has too much aeration.

Current thinking is that lawns should be aerated from at least four, to as many as six times a year. A lawn that is regularly aerated year-to-year needs it less often than one that has been neglected, and excess thatch, as well as compaction, may call for more frequent aeration.

This is our first season to get into aeration and so

far it has gone well. It is another pot of gold for us, it seems!

For supplemental information, books, and advertising ideas on aeration, please visit:
www.LawnBusinessResources.com

TIPS
- Water (or have your client water) the area that you are going to be aerating the night before. This will soften the soil to allow for maximum core penetration.
- Before beginning, map out any obstructions such as sprinkler heads or drains.
- Be sure and cover every inch of the lawn. Go over high traffic areas more than once to ensure good coverage.
- After aerating, water the lawn and apply fertilizer. This will promote growth and allow grass to compete with weed growth.

When it comes to pricing, here are a few methods to get you started on estimating:
1. By the hour. You can charge your hourly rate plus whatever equipment costs you have. In this case I would recommend an average of about $60 per hour.
2. For residential you could charge 2-3 times the regular mowing price.
3. Charge by the square foot. From my experience somewhere between $9-$14 per 1000 sq. feet
*None of the above are set in stone. They are to give you an idea to get you started.

Dethatching

If you look right beneath the grass and there is a layer of dead grass that seems to be all matted together, you may need to dethatch. Thatch is a layer of dead stems, roots and clippings between the soil's surface and the green vegetation. Thatch can deprive your lawn of the vital nutrients it needs to be healthy. A thatch layer of one-half inch or more also keeps water and air from entering the grass roots and provides the perfect breeding environment for insects and disease.

Dethatching is a process that removes accumulated thatch using rigid wire tines that lift thatch debris to the surface for removal. Once this build-up is eliminated air, water, and nutrients can flow more freely to the roots, rejuvenating a lifeless lawn.

Dethatching may cause some minor damage or browning to the turf. This shouldn't last too long, and the lawn will look much better in the end. To help speed the recovery of the lawn, all thatch should be removed using a lawn vacuum, blower or hand rake. Once you have cleaned up all the thatch, you can fertilize and use herbicide to prevent the growth of weeds. This will give the lawn the nutrients it needs to regain a green, lush appearance in no time.

Overseeding

Lawns that are thinning, have bare patches, or barely have any grass at all require some aggressive renovation techniques. Lawns like this may be revived by overseeding with a powered lawn seeder. These work by using a hopper that drops a measured amount of seed (set by the operator) while the lawn seeder plants the seed by blending them into the ground through the action of the rotating knife blades.

Water the lawn thoroughly as soon as overseeding is complete and then lightly each day until the seed germinates. Once the grass has sprouted, water regularly to encourage deeper growth.

For best results, I recommend overseeding in two applications. The second application should be made at a 45-degree angle to the first (basically a criss-cross pattern). You'll notice a distinct crosshatch pattern in the lawn as the blades of the overseeder cut rows of and inserts seeds into the turf beneath the topsoil.

For a list of manufacturers of powered lawn seeders, please visit:
www.LawnBusinessResources.com

Pine Straw and Pine Mulch

Putting in pine straw or mulch is a good money maker as an add-on business, as well. Depending on where you are located, you may offer other types of ground cover in addition to pine straw or mulch.

Check around your area on prices. There are two things to consider here:

1. Do you want bagged or loose mulch?

We prefer to buy bagged mulch. It works out cheaper (than buying by the cubic yard) for us by the time we figure in labor to pick it up, deliver it, and spread it. Another reason we prefer to buy in bags is that it eliminates waste and cleanup of mulch pieces on the job site. With bulk mulch, there will be drippings of mulch everywhere you move it, load and unload the wheelbarrow, etc. You can't avoid it. Buying bagged mulch eliminates this.

2. Is your job too large to do manually?

There are more and more companies specializing in mulch installs using blower trucks. This is not feasible for smaller jobs, but when you get large jobs it can be a life saver. You can work out a deal to simply make a phone call and have the mulch installed for you. You make money and never touch a thing!

If you are in an area where you can use pine straw, it is an even bigger money maker for us. We can buy it for only $3.00 a bale but charge a good bit for installation.

Pine straw will look good for quite a while once installed. It is not only cheaper for us to buy, but it is quite a bit cheaper for our customers. Given the choice (and quoted a price), most will go with the straw.

TIP: How to determine cubic yards for mulch: Take the number of square feet of the bed(s) and multiply that by the depth you need the mulch. Divide that number by 27.

NOTE: The industry average for installing mulch is 1.2 hours per cubic yard!

How to price mulching:

I would charge about $65 - $75 per cubic yard installed. DO NOT tell the customer a per-bag charge or any amount like it. They want their property mulched and that is what you should give them a TOTAL price on. If you start giving them a per bag price they will start thinking about running to the local home center and buying it themselves. Then they'll try to talk you into installing it. Don't say I didn't warn you!

Concrete Curbing

In some areas, this is huge. There is one neighborhood we service where almost every house has some of this curbing. The curbing machines I've seen are all about the same.

The idea and concept was started by Richard Eagleton, a guy from Australia, in 1973. I wonder if he knew how big this business would become?

You don't have to perform this service yourself. You can partner with a company that does it and get a referral fee or a % of the profit.

If you decide to get into this business yourself, the profits are pretty high. In my neck of the woods, you can get $3.50 a running foot for this. There's a company in our town that only does this type of curbing. They cover about a 100 mile radius from here, and the owner nets over $100,000 from his curbing business.

> For a list of manufacturers or supplemental information on concrete curbing, please visit:
> www.LawnBusinessResources.com

Hydroseeding

Hydroseeding is a process of planting grass that's fast, economical, and very efficient. It is a good bit cheaper than sodding and is more effective than traditional seeding.

This service will require special equipment. Once you have a hydroseeding machine, the process is started by mixing mulch, seed, fertilizer, and water in the tank. The mix is sprayed on the ground and provides the proper environment for good seed germination.

Hydroseeding machines come in all sizes. Some of the newer, smaller machines make it possible for you to get started in this business with a reasonable investment.

Planting Seasonal Flowers

We make a good bit of supplemental income by planting seasonal flowers in the fall and in the spring. Before starting, you will need to get familiar with the flowers that grow best in your area and the times of year to plant them.

To market this service, I have a postcard I send out near the times of the year when we plant. The postcards go out to our existing customers. Planting the flowers is great money, and I'm already there doing other work in most cases.

This is not a hard sale. Most people want their lawn to look as good as it can, and the colorful flowers only add to the curb appeal. I price these on a per plant basis. I will get around $2 or so per plant for small flowers, etc.

Installing Landscape Ponds and Fountains

This segment of the market continues to grow. The ponds and small waterfalls are very popular. Waterfalls, water gardens, fishponds all make great add-ons to an existing business.

Our local irrigation supply company handles all the supplies needed to get into this business. I would not suggest that you buy the materials from a normal home improvement store. Your local irrigation supplier will be more knowledgeable and will have better quality materials in most cases.

For more information and a list of seminars on this topic, please visit:
www.LawnBusinessResources.com

Cleaning out Gutters

This is a fabulous money maker! Cleaning gutters is something almost every homeowner hates to do. I can clean out the gutters on most any house with my backpack blower in about 10 minutes. That said, this can be a messy way to do this because all the leaves you blow out of the gutters will end up all over the ground. You then have to clean up the mess you made!

I generally get $50 or so to clean out the average houses gutters. It takes less than an hour to clean them out and get up all of the debris. It can be good to package this with fall leaf cleanup, as the debris cleanup and leaf cleanup are the same process.

If the roof is too steep to get on to use the blower, I use my shop vac and an extension. This takes longer, but the cleanup afterward is minimal. Either way, it is good money and not a lot of work to offer this service.

Notes:

Chapter Seven:

Business Sense

"Why is it that with all the information available today on how to be successful in small business, so few people really are?"

-Michael Gerber

Adding a Helper

Hopefully it will not be too long until you will need to add a helper (or two) to your growing business. Depending on where you are located, you may have several options for getting help. I'm lucky and have two colleges near me. We use students to help during the summer when we are the busiest. You can also employ high school students, but be sure you are adhering to all rules regarding employment of minors.

It's a lot of hassle for me to keep up with payroll, etc., so I let an accountant do this for me. I give her the number of hours worked and the hourly rate of each employee and she does the payroll and writes the checks. You can do payroll yourself with a little help, but I think my time is better spent doing other things (like getting new customers)!

Whenever I have someone working for me I also get workers comp for them (I mentioned this in the insurance section in Chapter One). It doesn't cost that much for the lawn care industry, and I feel a lot better knowing they are covered in case something happens.

When I am hiring, I tend to see two types of people:

1. People who are great workers but seem to have no aspirations of starting their own lawn care business.
2. People who are outgoing and might try to start their own business in a year or so.

There is nothing wrong with either type of person, I just like to know which one I am dealing with. No matter what, I have anyone who helps me sign a no-compete contract. This says they won't approach any of my customers for 2 years after they quit working for me. If they don't want to sign it they don't work for me.

I do my best to treat people fairly and also reward hard work. I will occasionally buy lunch for employees or do something to show them I appreciate all they do. It makes a huge difference when you have employees who are happy to be working for you. Don't you like to feel appreciated? They do, too.

Before you add an employee, you need to get with your accountant and figure out what your true costs will be. If you hire someone for $10 an hour, it will really cost you more like $17 or so by the time you add taxes, workers comp, etc.

Time Is Money.
How Much Money Are You Making?

I have to get this rant off my chest before we can move on...

There are some people that just don't understand this concept. Time is money, no matter what you are doing. Say you can pay someone to paint a room for $100 (and you know they do good work). The same room might take you half a day to do yourself. Would you save $100 if you did it yourself? NO! You would lose money because you could have been doing what you do best (taking care of lawns) and making $60 + an hour! If it took you 4 hours, you lost $140 ($240 you could have made minus the $100 you would have paid them).

If you disagree with me about this, you are one of the people who still do not get it! Let me put it this way—if you make more money doing what you do, you should pay someone to do the task for you!

As you grow your business you will need to delegate more and more. This will allow you to spend more time growing your business. I have seen businesses fail simply because the owner felt that they needed to do it all. Don't fall into this faulty way of thinking!

*If they don't fail outright, most
businesses fail to fully achieve
their potential. That's because the
person who owns the business
doesn't truly know how to build a
company that works without him
or her...which is the key.
-Michael Gerber*

Setting a Yearly Income Goal

I know I have a section on goals, but I wanted to make this section separate. This section refers to goals strictly centered around your yearly income. Here's how to figure out what you need to do to reach your income goals. Let's say you want to clear $80,000 this year. You know there are 40 hours in each standard workweek x 50 weeks a year (2 weeks off for vacation time, etc.). That's 2000 hours you have to work with. Some time will be lost to various tasks, and you can't help this. I'd figure on having 1800 good, solid hours to reach your goal.

Now you take the $80,000 goal and divide it by 1800 hours. This shows you that you need to be doing tasks worth at least $45.00 an hour. You obviously can't mow all 1800 hours, but there are things you can do. You need to constantly be doing the things that bring in money. As you grow, have employees do the things that don't justify your $45/hour rate. For example, you can have two helpers mowing for you, etc. while you are out getting more new clients or selling a new irrigation job.

Ideally, to reach your goal, you should be doing work that's worth $45 an hour on average. You should also be making money, each hour, for each person you have working for you. Additionally, you should be making money off of materials for additional services such as mulch, flowers, etc. If you do these things, meeting your income goal for the year should be no problem. Once you understand how income goals work, you can start working toward your desired income with a clearly defined path.

Lawn Care Time Sheet

Customer	Date	Started	Finished	Services Performed	Bill Total

Using Software to Keep Up With It All

http://www.LawnProSoftware.com

In case you didn't know, I am a little partial to LawnPro software. It is my software, after all! I created it to be affordable and to help manage your lawn care business in the most effective way.

LawnPro can do the following and more:

› Keep up with customers you need to mow each day and print a list each day for each crew member.

› Be able to delay or cancel servicing a customer as needed, due to the weather, scheduling conflict, customer request, etc.

› Choose how you will bill someone (per visit, per month, etc.).

› Create, save, and print invoices

› Generate reports such as income and expense, sales by customer, etc. so you know how your business is doing and can make decisions accordingly.

› Print proposals and contracts with your customer's information auto-filled.

› Keep up with past-due amounts and add it to the next invoice.

You can get a single-user copy of LawnPro for under $100! Visit www.lawnprosoftware.com to get more information or to purchase your copy today!

16 Tips for Your Lawn Care Business

Here is a list of some tips I think you may enjoy. Who knows...one of these may save your workday!

1.   Engage the clutch on your mower at the lowest RPM you can without killing the engine. It will be a lot easier on your mower. You don't rev your truck up as high as you can before putting it in drive, do you? Why would you do that to your mower???

2.   Similar to tip #1, don't disengage your clutch while running at full RPM, either. Disengage your clutch at idle speed.

Don't slide a gas can across the bed liner in a truck. It causes static electricity to build up!

3.   Keep an extra set of blades and belts for your mowers with you at all times. This can save you from having to go back to your lawn care dealer if you break down.

4.   Buy a portable air tank and keep fix-a-flat and a patch kit. A spare tire mounted and aired up would be even better if you have a big enough truck / trailer. A flat tire can kill a couple of work hours for you if you have to stop to have it fixed...

5.   You know to keep an extra spool of trimmer line with you, but I like to keep a spare trimmer head with me, too. It doesn't cost that much, and it saves a trip to the dealer if something should happen while I am out working.

6.   Carry some wasp spray with you. You can be a hero for your customer! I have had to get rid of wasps on more than one occasion for customers. They were very surprised and very happy that I could take care of it for them.

7.   Check and make sure all car and house windows are closed BEFORE you start blowing off the lawn or driveway. I've blown dust all over the inside of a truck before I realized all the windows were open.

8.   Keep plenty of business cards and door hangers with you. There is always time to market your business!

9.   Carry a tool box with you and make sure you have all the tools you may need to do quick repairs on your equipment.

10.   I've mentioned this repeatedly, but it is worth repeating. ALWAYS wear hearing and eye protection!

11.   Make sure your equipment is secured to your trailer. Check the safety chains that secure your trailer to the truck.

12.   Carry a copy of your business license, pesticide and any other certifications you might need to show someone who inquires.

13.   When you are finished with a sprayer release the pressure on it. I have accidentally stepped on the wand of a sprayer and sprayed out weed killer. If this was facing the wrong direction it could have been very bad.

14.   Always carry an eye wash kit and a well-stocked first aid kit.

15.   Lock equipment down any time you are not using it. If you leave something sitting out, it only takes a second for someone to drive by and grab it.

16.   Fuel up your equipment at the end of the day. It makes getting started the next day a lot smoother.

Suggested Reading

I like to read and learn daily. I don't think you can ever learn too much! I have tons of books I think you would benefit from. I've listed them in the book and reading section at www.LawnBusinessResources.com

Bookmark that site and check it often. I update this every week. I usually read at least one book a week or listen to an audio book in my truck or on my iPod.

Sites to Visit

There are a couple of sites I would recommend you can visit on the internet.
They are: (in no particular order)
www.LawnCare-Business.com
www.LawnServicing.com
www.LawnSite.com
www.LawnProSoftware.com

Some good magazines to subscribe to are:
Outdoor Power Equipment
Irrigation & Green Industry
Landscape and Irrigation
Landscape Management
Power Equipment Trade
Grounds Maintenance
Lawn and Landscape Magazine
PRO Magazine

You can find links to all of this and more at
www.LawnBusinessResources.com

Final Thoughts

Well, you have made it to the end of my guide on starting and running your own lawn care business. I hope you have learned a few things and are already on your way to growing your business. As I mentioned in the beginning of the guide, don't limit yourself to just mowing. There is a world full of opportunities out there! And remember, the only place you will find <u>success</u> before <u>work</u> is in the dictionary.

Keep working at it and do more than is expected of you and you will succeed.

Take care,

Patrick

Made in the USA
Lexington, KY
03 October 2016